MISS SARAH'S GUIDE TO

ETIQUETTE

FOR DOGS
& THEIR PEOPLE

D1511742

Miss Sarah's Guide to ETIQUETTE FOR DOGS & THEIR PEOPLE

by Sarah Hodgson

with Arthur Greenwald

featuring illustrations by Patricia Storms

Wiley Publishing, Inc.

For general information on our other products and services or to obtain technical support please contact our Customer Care Department within the U.S. at (800) 762-2974, outside the U.S. at (317) 572-3993 or fax (317) 572-4002.

Wiley also publishes its books in a variety of electronic formats. Some content that appears in print may not be available in electronic books. For more information about Wiley products, please visit our web site at www.wiley.com.

Library of Congress Cataloging-in-Publication Data is available from the publisher upon request.

ISBN-13: 978-0-7645-9988-0

ISBN-10: 0-7645-9988-7

Printed in the United States of America

10 9 8 7 6 5 4 3 2 1

Book design by Melissa Auciello-Brogan
Book production by Wiley Publishing, Inc. Composition Services

A special curtsy and a tip of the hat to the two women whose
wisdom and grace inspired every stage of this project.
We dedicate this book to our friends, Rosemarie Lee and Nancy Shalek.

—Sarah and Arthur

ACKNOWLEDGMENTS

We're grateful for the many whose kindness or careers have touched our lives and inspired this book.

An enormous hug of gratitude goes to the team who championed this project. With unfailing courtesy, editor Pam Mourouzis shepherded this book from the first tentative proposal through each copy revision. We also thank Jenn Connolly, whose early ideas shaped the book's direction. And we're delighted to work alongside illustrator Patricia Storms, whose artistry graces nearly every page.

Thanks to Sarah's clients, human and canine, who have helped her to refine her methods over the years by sharing every success, setback, and solution.

Sarah is grateful to her beloved Aunt Carolyn, who offered an important life lesson: "Your manners define your character; you're known and judged by how you behave." Sarah strives to pass on that wisdom to her daughter, Lindsay—and to her dog, Whoopsie, as well.

Arthur's life is graced by the company of Traffic and Emily, two outstanding Dalmatian-Americans. He is grateful for the friendship and wisdom of the late Fred Rogers, who continues to inspire millions to kinder thoughts and actions.

All animal behaviorists owe a debt to William Cambell, Job Evans, and Barbara Woodhouse, whose work and writing elevated dog training from the show ring to its proper place in everyday life.

Finally, we tip our hats to the great ladies of American etiquette—Emily Post, Amy Vanderbilt, Letitia Baldridge, and Judith Martin. Each in her own way reminds us that kindness and courtesy never go out of style.

TABLE OF CONTENTS

ABOUT THE AUTHORS

"Miss Sarah" Hodgson is the author of seven dog training books, including *Puppies For Dummies, DogPerfect, PuppyPerfect,* and *Teach Yourself VISUALLY Dog Training.* Sarah has been a trainer of dogs and their people for over 20 years. Her celebrity clients include Katie Couric, Richard Gere, Glenn Close, Chazz Palmientieri, Chevy Chase, Lucie Arnaz, George Soros, Tommy Hilfiger, Tommy Mottola, and Bobby Valentine. She lives in Katonah, New York, with her daughter, Lindsay, and her black Lab, Whoopsie Daisy. For more information, visit Sarah's website: www.dogperfect.com.

Arthur Greenwald is an award-winning writer and producer, whose television programs have appeared on PBS, CBS, Lifetime, and the Sci-Fi Channel. He has served as a creative and strategic media consultant to a wide range of clients, including the Academy of Television Arts and Sciences, the Ad Council, Bloomberg Television, and Yale University. Greenwald lives in Studio City, California, with his Dalmatians, Traffic and Emily, who report that Arthur's training is "coming along nicely."

INTRODUCTION

*A*n etiquette book for dogs? It makes a lot of sense when you think about it. Although people have been domesticating dogs for millions of years, our canine companions are still a little rough around the edges. Here, finally, is a book that offers useful behavioral tips in the broader context of common courtesy.

Miss Sarah's Guide to Etiquette for Dogs & Their People is designed to help you and your dog better understand and respect each other's wishes, and to interact politely with the world at large. This book provides lots of tips for curbing your dog's misguided impulses, as well as behavioral insights to help you modify your own. With consistent practice, you and your dog will soon create an orderly environment that extends from your home to practically anywhere you choose to visit.

A note on gender: While etiquette experts continue to debate the proper use of masculine and feminine pronouns, I have eschewed the awkward repetition of "he or she" in favor of using only "he" or "she" in alternating sections. An imperfect solution but, I hope, a polite one.

I am already at work on companion materials, and I would love to include your comments and questions. For more information, please visit www.dogperfect.com.

WHERE GOOD MANNERS BEGIN

*I*f your dog is ill-mannered, I'm afraid you have only yourself to blame. Although he may be blissfully unaware how his behavior reflects upon his species, his behavior also reflects upon you. We humans are ultimately responsible for canine etiquette. After all, good manners begin at home. Happily, even the most ill-mannered dog usually wants to please his humans. All it takes is a little time.

Yes, I realize that you are busy, but good manners are also a practical choice. Will your dog jump up and startle visitors or learn to sit attentively near the door? Will you teach your dog to expect food only in a bowl or inadvertently reward counter-cruising by tossing tidbits from the table? Will you watch helplessly as your home furnishings gradually disintegrate or direct your dog toward acceptable chew toys? Whether it is measured by enjoyment or economics, dog etiquette is well worth the effort. The time you spend now with your puppy or dog will instill a lifetime's worth of social graces.

We witness the value of dog etiquette anytime we enjoy the company of someone who has civilized her dog. This harmonious team of dog and owner communes comfortably on every level. How can you share in this synchronicity? Just consider life from your dog's perspective!

Remember, dear reader, that an ill-mannered dog is a confused dog. And that confusion is almost always caused by mixed signals—the most confusing of which is spoken language. At first, your dog understands English as well as the average American comprehends Urdu, which is to say not at all. Merely repeating your displeasure in a loud, angry tone does nothing to bridge this communication gap.

Fortunately, dogs *do* understand attention—especially winning notice from the top dog in the pack, which, in your household, I pray, is *you*. Again, consider the dog's perspective: No matter what behavior a dog displays upon arrival in a strange new home, he is automatically showered with attention and affection. A dog can only conclude that this love fest is the new norm. Then, just as he has developed a rather swelled head, the new owners randomly "bark" their displeasure in that strange language of theirs. To the dog, this makes no sense!

Strive to remember that dogs crave our attention, whether positive or negative. In fact, they rarely distinguish between the two. The key to dog etiquette is how you bestow your attention. With practice, you will learn to reward only your dog's good manners with your attention and interaction. Almost without fail, he will repeat that good behavior. This fundamental concept bears repeating, and so I shall repeat it—frequently throughout this guide.

Your dog is a social creature. By his very nature, he will want to join you whenever possible. But if he races freely about your home, odds are you have inadvertently conditioned this mischief by responding to it. Attention strikes again! To correct this problem, you will need to redirect his jaunts by placing him on a leash. After all, he has no clue how to manage his freedom until you guide him. The leash will not merely restrain your dog, but also calm him by imparting a reassuring sense of order.

Your next step in creating a civilized home life is to identify the rooms in which your dog is welcome. In each of these rooms, establish a "welcome zone"—someplace easy to find but out of the flow of traffic, such as in a comfy corner or against a wall. Spruce up each zone with a mat or bedding, along with a favorite chew to occupy idle time.

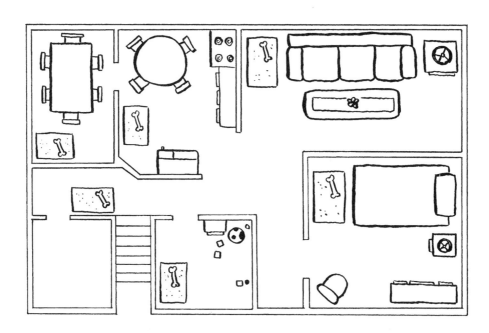

Bring your dog along with you whether you are watching television, resting, or working. As you enter each room, send him to his designated area with a consistent phrase, such as "Settle." Of course, he still doesn't understand your language, but over time, repetition will link the sound to the action in your dog's mind. Do make sure that your dog has been fed, has exercised, and has pottied before expecting him to sit still.

Spending this time together provides conditioning opportunities not to be missed. Your dog is learning to follow your lead, contain his impulses around your home, and adjust to your rhythm. His reward? The pleasure of your company.

Note: A floor mat can be placed on furniture, specifying exactly which cushion is his.

Miss Sarah Says

How would you like to be confined to a cluttered space with nowhere to relax? Wouldn't you rather be welcomed into a room with a comfortable chair and an activity to occupy your time? Your dog is no different.

1. Help your dog recognize his own areas in each room, just as you would for a visitor or a child.

2. Install comfortable bedding in a predetermined space in each room that you share.

3. Spruce up this space with a favorite chew or toy.

4. To reinforce the desired behavior, send your dog to his place when you enter the room together, saying "Settle" and then "Stay" once he is in his area.

5. If an activity raises your dog's curiosity, secure him to an immovable object, such as a piece of furniture, with a 3-foot leash to discourage his wanderings.

   If he throws a tantrum, consider a head collar, a humane and safe way to condition calmness. Head collars can be purchased at most pet stores; ask a sales associate to help you select one that is appropriate for your dog.

Your dog may take days or weeks to cooperate. Teaching a dog to keep still in one location is like teaching a child to sit quietly at the dinner table: It takes practice and patience, but it will come together. Make sure that you offer an appropriate chew toy to help your dog displace his energies or anxiety.

Of course, you must set realistic expectations. A puppy's attention span is nearly nil. A puppy under 6 months of age can be expected to occupy himself for only fifteen minutes at a time, but that duration will gradually increase. Concentration improves with age and maturity.

Miss Sarah Says

If you are using this book to help civilize a new puppy, you are in an excellent position. He will learn to behave properly within his first year of life. Good behavior makes everyone happy—especially your puppy.

As always, my best advice for you is this: Your attention is the most effective reward. Addressing your puppy or dog when he is exhibiting uncivilized manners will only confuse him. Your animation and frustration will be misunderstood as confrontational play, and your puppy will likely repeat any behavior that gleans a response. In the same vein, if you react to your dog when he is sitting calmly on his bed or playing with a toy, your attention will reinforce this good behavior. His repeat performance will be guaranteed— whether it is bad or good.

Note: Do not attempt to secure your puppy on leash until he is at least 12 weeks of age and has shown that he will accept the leash. Also be mindful of interpreting his signals—puppies often fidget when they need something, such as food, water, or potty time.

In the beginning, your behavior with your dog may be inconsistent. This is perfectly normal. After all, you are learning, too. Try to observe your own mistakes and learn from them. Be mindful of how your actions affect your dog. Forgive your dog's transgressions, and I shall forgive you yours.

A dog who displays the social graces, who has learned to sit still and occupy himself while the humans around him are busy, is a fine ambassador for his species. This is a dog you can brag about—a source of pride who is soon promoted from mere pet to full-fledged family member. This is my wish for each and every dog, especially yours.

SAY PLEASE

All dogs, regardless of age, must learn manners in order to be appreciated and accepted in polite society. Unruly behavior is embarrassing, although most dogs are unaware of our disapproval. By the very nature of her species, a dog will repeat whatever action gets a reaction. If it is jumping, then so be it. If you have something else in mind, dear reader, then you must offer clear direction and deliver your message consistently.

Ideally, your dog will learn to solicit interaction by utilizing the canine gesture for "please," and that is to sit and look up. As ever, when your dog behaves correctly, her greatest reward is your fond attention. How appropriate to acknowledge her polite behavior with an affectionate "Thank you!"

The alternative, of course, is unacceptable. A dog who grabs things out of someone's hand is pushy, even dangerous. You would not accept such behavior from a human. Climbing onto a countertop to scrounge for food is equally boorish. Nosing through a purse or a shopping bag? Rude, rude, rude! A dog is not a vulture. And a dog who seeks a visitor's attention by leaping at his face or prodding his crotch is reprehensible. Alas, without your intervention, the poor dog knows no other way to interact.

Miss Sarah Says

If your dog resorts to counter-cruising, facial leaps, and crotch-sniffing to get attention, she is not completely to blame. Perhaps you have admonished her and are perplexed that she won't stop. The reason is that she craves interaction and will do anything to elicit your attention—even negative attention satisfies this urge. Help your dog learn more respectful ways to communicate. This simple exercise will get the ball rolling.

Start in a quiet room with a handful of kibble or a favorite toy.

1. Hold the toy or kibble at arm's length, above your dog's head.
2. If she leaps, lift the toy or kibble straight up and out of reach. Be silent. Look away from her.
3. Lower the toy or kibble to its original position above her head.
4. If she jumps, lift it again. Repeat this process over and over until she tires and sits.
5. If she does not sit, position her by squeezing her waist muscles just below her ribs.
6. As soon as she cooperates by sitting still, drop the object to reward her.

If you notice that your dog will not sit without a treat, do not repeat the direction, lest you sound like a broken record. Simply position her quickly and then reward her.

Although waiting quietly can be a difficult skill for any species to grasp, your dog will master it over time. If she displays "impatience" by pacing, whining, or fidgeting, direct her to "Sit," positioning her if necessary. Instruct her to "Sit" before opening a door or gate, and make her wait a moment before allowing her to enter or exit the car. Withhold toys, water, treats, or affection until your dog is, in effect, saying please. If your dog is interested in a bag or a surface, insist that she "Sit," and then either remove the temptation or let her sniff it. Do remember that dogs "see" with their noses, not with their eyes. Forbidding sniffing may cause frustration and lead to stealing.

Your dog wants to stay connected to you and be a part of the household activity. Often, dogs mirror human behavior almost like toddlers do. If you are focused on the counter, she will want to have a look, too. If you are poking through your purse, she'll want to nose right along with you. These are signs of natural bonding—you should feel honored that your gestures are so revered. Although I agree that this behavior presents you with a dilemma, do not reprimand your dog for the show of devotion. Instead, focus your attention on teaching her a better approach.

THE FOUR-PAW RULE

Inconveniencing others by allowing your dog to jump up on them as a form of greeting is socially unacceptable. What's more, it is unfair to the dog, who will be ostracized by polite society.

Ironically, your efforts to teach your dog to keep four paws on the floor may be undermined by your own friends and family, some of whom may actually encourage your dog to jump in greeting. How confusing! For the sake of civility and consistency, you will have to teach everyone the Four-Paw Rule, whether they walk on four legs or two.

It is not surprising that your dog is so attuned to household activities. After all, dogs rarely have busy schedules, so human comings and goings are vastly entertaining. But unlike people, who recognize and acknowledge each other visually, your dog is near-sighted and odor-dependent. He identifies others through close facial engagement and scent. Although it is unacceptable, jumping up is an understandable canine behavior, as your dog's impulse is to take a closer look. Even if your dog startles a visitor, please remember your own manners and be kind. Rather than isolate him, show him a more reasonable gesture to invite acknowledgement.

Whether you are opening the door for yourself or to welcome a visitor, teach your dog one of three perfectly civilized greeting options. Each is a refreshing change from jumping up and is a more reasonable gesture to invite recognition. Consider your dog's personality:

- Is he a Giver? This fellow displaces his anxiety on a toy or other object, often bringing it to visitors as a peace offering, sometimes inviting a game of fetch.

- Is he a Belly Flasher? This little angel greets company with an invitation for a belly scratch.

- Is he a Contained Canine? The most restrained of the three types, this dog greets newcomers simply by sitting down, often at the perfect angle to invite facial interaction.

Select one to begin, although you may try all three if you're unsure of which option will best suit your dog. Use your choice to manage your dog's behavior whenever and wherever he greets people.

THE GIVER

If your dog is active and engaged, this may be the ideal greeting ritual to vent his enthusiasm. The goal is to teach your dog to carry, toss, or fetch a favored object when greeting new arrivals. Help him learn to parade his proud possession to win the admiration of anyone who enters the house—including you. Although visitors may briefly consider him hyperactive, most will feel flattered to receive the "gift" of your dog's ball or toy. They will recognize the implied invitation to play and will happily bestow the attention your dog craves.

Miss Sarah Says

Do you think that your dog may be a Giver? Here is an exercise to help you find out.

1. Choose an object that your dog holds in high regard. In my house, it is a tennis ball—the more worn the better.

2. Whatever the treasured object, purchase plenty of them and place them throughout your home. Invite your dog to play whenever the opportunity presents itself. Select a special word or phrase, such as "Ball," to signal your intentions.

3. Gather at least five of the special objects and keep them handy in a basket by your main doorway.

4. Each time someone enters through the main door (yourself included), use your special word (for example, "Ball!") to highlight the object as you toss one on the floor.

5. Ignore your four-footed friend until he either has calmed down or approaches with the toy.

THE BELLY FLASHER

Perhaps your dog's favorite position is belly up, practically guaranteeing a rub. If so, here is a method that is almost foolproof. Encourage your dog to greet visitors by lowering his head and rolling onto his back to receive a quick tummy scratch. Throughout the day, use your special word or phrase (such as "Belly up!") to encourage his submissive posture. Teach him that four splayed paws and two serenely closed eyelids will buy extra belly time.

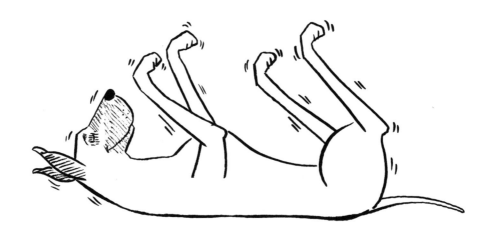

Miss Sarah Says

Do you think your dog may be a Belly Flasher? Here's how to be sure:

1. Each time you scratch your dog's belly during the day, highlight this action with a special word or phrase, such as "Belly up!"

2. Ignore your dog's excited behavior for several minutes each time you return home.

3. After he has calmed himself, kneel down and say "Belly up!" as you greet him with a tummy rub.

Practice this technique with family, friends, and new visitors. Your dog will quickly conclude that this is the appropriate way to greet nearly everyone.

THE CONTAINED CANINE

If your dog is generally unimpressed by the comings and goings in your household but is jumping up in order to impress family and friends, then your task is far simpler. How can you tell? Well, if your dog is excited for a few minutes but calms down quickly, then his jumping is mostly for show. It is little more than a display he puts on to get attention.

Teach your dog to approach all visitors on four paws and, if he desires interaction, to sit and wait for it. A sitting dog angles his face on a direct plane to a nearby human's. No one will be able to resist rewarding his eager expression with a pat or a kiss!

Miss Sarah Says

Are you guilty of sending your dog a mixed signal or two? Do you like the jumping when it suits you but find yourself reprimanding your dog for greeting visitors in the same way? Think long and hard about how confusing this is for him. Instead, guide your dog along in this new regimen:

1. When you return home, ignore your dog at first.

2. If he jumps or gyrates out of habit, brace him into a sitting position. To brace your dog properly, clip your right thumb over his collar, pointing toward the floor, and fan your fingers across his chest. For extra leverage, use your left index finger and thumb to hold his midsection. This is especially helpful when greeting guests or strangers.

3. As you greet him, repeat a verbal cue such as "Say hello!"

Follow this routine with visitors, too.

Note: You can break the Four-Paw Rule from time to time. Simply teach your dog to jump on cue. When he is calm, say "Up, up" as you lure him up onto you with a snack or gently lift him onto your lap. Don't encourage jumping too much, though, or your dog will not be able to follow your logic.

DOORWAY ETIQUETTE

Although you think of your front door as a mere entryway, from your dog's perspective, it is the portal to power. It is also the opening to her den. To a dog, whoever controls access to your home rules the roost. In the name of all that is civilized, let's make sure that it is you!

Whether you are preparing for a walk or answering the doorbell, allowing your dog to make a mad dash for the door is simply abhorrent. Worse, it tells your dog that she is in charge. If you allow this behavior, your permissiveness may encourage belligerence—all the more so if you inadvertently reward the commotion with your attention. Now is the time to reclaim your position as gatekeeper by changing your dog's perception. Never follow her through the front door; always lead her. Once your authority has been recognized, you can build upon it to address a host of issues. If left unchecked, "door dashing" can escalate to even more boorish canine habits, including running away, territorial aggression, and even potty confusion. Let's examine each of these problems in detail.

- *Running away:* Some dogs are born escape artists. They dash out the door and may not return for hours, or even days. You frantically search or await your dog's return, while she enjoys blissful freedom. It is best to discourage this behavior *before* it starts. By taking charge of the doorway, you communicate that you are the leader of all adventures. Like the famous credit card slogan goes, your dog will learn never to leave home without you.

- *Barking and patrolling:* What you call home is a den to your dog. Unless you take charge, she may appoint herself head of homeland security. She will consider it her proud duty to guard your living space and the land around it. A friendly dog may welcome suspicious strangers as long-lost friends. More cautious dogs may aggressively confront dear Aunt Edna before you usher her through the door.

- *Housetraining issues:* Dogs generally do not like to soil their living space. If your dog dashes in and out of the doorway, however, she may not grasp the difference between indoors and out, and will certainly not develop respect for your definition of either. This is especially true if your dog is small and your home is large—a far-off room may seem so distant that your dog won't perceive it as part of her living space.

Fear not, dear reader! All this is easier than it may sound. For one thing, most dogs would rather *not* serve as the gatekeeper. After all, playing that role is exhausting. Besides, aggressive doorway behavior provides a clue to the solution—it suggests your dog's deeper frustration over her general lack of control. You can overcome this problem by establishing clear rituals for all the usual events that take place at your door, including how you enter and exit, what happens when the doorbell rings, and how visitors are welcomed. You will find specific instructions for each activity on the pages ahead.

If your dog goes bonkers each time you depart or return, or when the doorbell rings, she likely views herself as responsible for your social calendar as well as your safety. This, again, is a job your dog would happily resign from. Once you actively take charge of all doorway activity, she will likely abandon her guardlike behavior and defer to your judgment.

Early manners last a lifetime. Lucky is the puppy who learns this lesson from the start.

Miss Sarah Says

Would you allow a person to drag you out the door by your shirtsleeve? Certainly not! So, for civility's sake, do not let your dog do so. Remember, you must always be the leader of your dog's "pack." At the doorway and elsewhere, leaders lead.

When going out for air, routinely lead your dog by preceding her through the door. Never let her pull you out; not only is this dangerous, but it also may give her the impression that you are following her lead. Safety is a task you must manage for the both of you. Remember, even a small dog can pull you off balance. Follow this procedure each time you pass through the door:

1. As you bring your dog to the door, instruct "Wait."

2. Stand still for a moment.

3. If your dog pulls you forward, tug her back inside again and again, until she either stands still or looks up. You are teaching her that she must wait for your okay before venturing forth.

4. When she does pause, say "Okay," and then walk first out the door, encouraging her to "Follow," as described later in this book.

Employ the same method at car doors and when approaching stairways.

When company arrives, it is only natural for your dog to want to check out the new visitors. After all, these people are coming into your communal "den." Yet while I respect a dog's instincts, courtesy demands that you remain in charge of all greeting rituals, lest they veer out of control. Dashing about and barking are inherently rude, and often terrifying to guests who don't recognize a friendly dog's exuberance. (Protective dogs will take a more assertive approach.) Please make every effort to extend your control when company calls.

This is best accomplished by organizing your doorway space. Direct your dog to a specific place as you redirect her energy to an appropriate toy. Ignore wild outbursts. When she is calm, introduce her to visitors, using her leash to enable gentle restraint should she behave inappropriately. Use this routine whenever the doorbell rings, gradually phasing off the leash as your dog learns to mind your direction.

Establish proper etiquette by creating a special place by your door where your dog can wait when you leave, when you come home, or when company arrives. Now orchestrate some practice sessions:

1. Secure a short leash to an immovable object, using a mat or rug to define your dog's place.

2. Place a basket of toys or a handful of kibble nearby.

3. Ask a friend, posing as a visitor, to knock on the door or ring the bell.

4. Before you open the door, bring your dog to her designated area and direct her to go to her "Place."

5. If your dog won't stay, secure her to the leash and instruct "Stay." (Leave a toy out for her to vent her energies. Attend to her only after she is calm or is interacting with the toy, at which point you may reward her with a food treat.)

Repeat this exercise until your dog displays signs of full cooperation. Be patient and alert. It may take five repetitions to notice any change in her behavior, and twenty to elicit even an iota of cooperation. Reprogramming takes time, but it is always effective in the end. The behavior you pay attention to will always be repeated.

Even courteous people can be disruptive. You and your dog may be making real head-way, and then—boom!—a surprise visitor arrives and inspires a manic outburst. Even if your guest appears to tolerate or even enjoy the chaos and/or jumping, you must stand firm and be consistent. Enlist cooperation by asking the visitor to ignore your dog as you provide a toy or other familiar object to help her regain her composure before you attempt to hold her still. Doing so will at least meet basic behavior standards and give everyone a chance to settle down. If your dog knows a trick or two, this is an ideal time to showcase her cleverness.

Miss Sarah Says

"Attention reinforces reaction. Attention reinforces reaction. Attention reinforces reaction. . . ." Repeat this mantra to all who will listen. If your dog loses control, do not reward her with a big reaction. Instead, pity her. Help her vent her energies with a toy or two. What she wants more than anything is to make a connection. Only after she has calmed herself should you greet her or introduce her. Before long, she will respect your direction, mirror your energy level, and greet guests calmly.

This simple exercise establishes a calm and civilized tone for the entire household and reinforces your role as "pack leader." Remember, dear reader: From your dog's perspective, whoever takes charge of the door rules the den.

DAILY CONSTITUTIONALS

ivilizing your dog takes energy and persistence. It is only natural to feel discouraged at the sight of a puddle or pile on your floor or carpet. Stop, take a deep breath, and stay focused on your long-term goal: a happy, harmonious household. Look beyond this unsightly mess to discover what your puppy or dog might be trying to convey.

Have you offered too much freedom too soon? Is he frustrated by rough handling, prolonged separation, or extenuating circumstances? Could his problem be physical—perhaps a bladder infection? Happily, dogs and even puppies are rarely messy by nature. Usually they can learn bladder control within a relatively short time if the lesson is simple and structured. Whether you prefer that your dog relieve himself outside or indoors on a paper or pad, the same rules apply: Reinforce a specific location at consistent times. Don't worry about overemphasizing this routine, especially not at first. Although some dogs learn quickly, your frequent repetition will make a lasting impression.

Miss Sarah Says

Regardless of your dog's reasoning, soiling your living space is more than merely distasteful; it is socially and hygienically unacceptable! When housetraining a dog of any age, three things are paramount:

- *Patience:* Your dog will learn at his own pace; some dogs get the system immediately, while others take weeks to learn it.

- *Repetition:* If you do not provide a routine, you cannot housetrain a dog. A scattered timetable is counterproductive. In the absence of consistency, your dog will develop his own routine, which may not coincide with yours.

- *Focus:* Make housetraining your top priority until your dog reliably potties when and where you direct him. Other lessons can wait. Limit your words to those that teach him where to potty.

To help your dog learn to regulate himself, establish a structured schedule—the more predictable the routine the better. A reasonable schedule for a mature dog includes feedings at 7am and 4pm and outings at 8am, 11:30am, 3pm, and 8pm. Of course, immature puppy bladders require more frequent outings.

Most dogs gravitate to a specific area and do not like to soil their living space. But if your home is large or your dog is small, trotting off to a distant room may seem to him like the great outdoors. While accidents are frustrating, please avoid scolding or berating your dog. Your anger will only serve to frighten or challenge him, neither of which is helpful when teaching impulse control. Help your dog focus on the larger goal. Keep him contained and supervise him. Cheer his successes, and watch his capacity to control his body improve along with his attitude.

If you have a puppy, let common sense be your guide. "Holding it" requires muscle control that has not yet developed. During active play, his bladder contents will shake; while napping, all matter navigates downward; and during isolation, physical pressure builds. Each of these conditions calls for release and necessitates a trip to the potty area.

Don't forget: The need to go potty is as important to your dog as drinking and eating. If you serve meals in a consistent location, your dog quickly learns where to go when he is hungry. The same rules apply to housetraining. Routinely take your puppy to his spot after every activity—eating, drinking, playing, or resting. He'll soon learn to monitor his own bladder and indicate his need to relieve himself.

Miss Sarah Says

One housetraining method to avoid is scattering newspapers about the floor. Doing so is unfair to the print media and quite confusing to your dog—not unlike placing several toilets around the kitchen and expecting your toddler to pick one. Instead, choose one quiet corner near the main room and bring your dog there often to show him where to go.

The same goes for outdoor locations. Select one small, specific potty area. Expecting your dog to go potty while touring the neighborhood is confusing and counterproductive. It is the equivalent of toilet-training a child by sending her door-to-door.

Lead your dog to a spot near the exit door and stand there until he goes. If he doesn't, perhaps he doesn't need to or he just isn't ready. After five minutes, isolate him inside, keeping him with you on a leash or in a crate or, if he's small enough, carrying him. Try again in ten to fifteen minutes.

Once your dog's routine has been established, he will likely devise a behavioral signal indicating that he needs to go potty. Some signals are more obvious than others. If your household routine follows the same path, your dog may telegraph his need to go out by racing between you and the door.

Other dogs are more subtle. If your dog stares longingly at the door as if willing it to open, you both may suffer the consequences of this silent approach. The solution is to teach an auxiliary signal:

- *Ringing a bell:* Hang a bell or chime at your dog's nose level and ring it each time you exit to go to his potty area. He will probably learn to ring it himself within a week or so. If he does not, secretly coat the bell lightly with peanut butter or another creamy spread. Bring him to the door at potty time and, as his licking rings the bell, open the door.

- *Barking:* If your dog is noisy by nature, teach him to bark when his need is pressing. Before each outing, make him wait at the door and encourage him to sound off, even if you have to bark along with him! As soon as he barks, open the door.

To fully housetrain your dog, you must understand him. A mature dog who has demonstrated bladder control still may use his urine to express anxiety or frustration or to mark territorial boundaries. Alas, this is not an occasion where turnabout is fair play.

As the de facto pack leader, you must avoid extreme or angry reactions, which will only strengthen his resolve. Instead, focus your frustration on an effective, lasting remedy. Win his cooperation with appropriate structure, confinement, and these helpful techniques:

- Teach him to follow your direction rather than to direct you. (The "Follow Me" section of this book contains many helpful tips.)

- Do not allow him to mark territory outside. Establish a specific spot for him to potty and lead him there before each walk. As you walk, teach him the skills addressed in the "Follow Me" section. When he pulls away to sniff or mark, tug the leash. You must consistently communicate that sniffing and marking are unacceptable indoors and out. After all, if he can mark outside, he will do it inside.

- If you see him sniffing an indoor area as if he is preparing to mark it, interrupt him with a loud sound like " Ep, ep!" and take him outside.

Some dogs mark indoors mainly to win your attention, even making brazen eye contact while urinating. This behavior tests both your patience and your acting skills. You must feign boredom and calmly walk away from the "accident." Later, when your dog is secluded, clean up and deodorize the soiled area. He will soon associate marking behavior with less attention, not more.

Miss Sarah Says

Your housetraining regimen is the cornerstone of canine courtesy. Therefore, let's review the key elements:

- Set aside your frustrations and befriend your dog. Extreme reactions will only increase his anxiety or strengthen his resolve. Patience, structure, and more patience will win him over.

- Choose a consistent one-word cue to direct your dog to his area. Each time his bladder presses, your familiar word, such as "Outside" or "Papers," will play in his head like an advertising jingle.

- Reinforce your dog's destination and mission by following a consistent path to his bathroom area.

- If a door or gate must be opened, consider hanging a bell or chime at your dog's nose level and ring it with him as you pass. Eventually, he will nose it on his own to alert you to his needs—a splendid signal!

- Limit fun and interaction until your dog has pottied. Organize and monitor all eating, drinking, and play activities to enable you to track his elimination habits.

Housetraining can be the most challenging, yet most rewarding, aspect of dog etiquette. It is so fundamental to your dog's social acceptance that we humans are eager to cheer any hint of bowel or bladder control. Ironically, our eagerness can send the wrong message. Coaxing, scolding, or, worse, yelling at your dog only bestows the inappropriate attention he craves. Don't assume that he "knows what he's done." Your dog is wholly incapable of human reasoning. You must appear calm and detached, offering praise and attention only after your dog eliminates at the proper time and place.

And while cleanliness is next to, well, dogliness, you must *never* clean up his accidents in front of him. It not only rewards his misdeed with inappropriate attention, but also instinctively reminds him of a mother dog cleaning his whelping box. Clean up all accidents only after your dog has been relocated. And because your dog has shown that he is not ready for this level of freedom, think about what else you can do to prevent future accidents.

You would never allow a toddler to roam the house without a diaper. Although doggy diapers do exist, a better plan involves steady surveillance or confinement, perhaps with the dog tethered to you by a leash. Watch for your dog's special potty signal, such as wandering away from an activity, sudden nipping, or sniffing about.

If your puppy is still having accidents, don't ask what the puppy is doing wrong. Instead, focus on what you are not doing right.

Finally, note that constant accidents may signal an infection or infestation. If your efforts to housetrain your dog meet with limited success, make an appointment with your dog's veterinarian.

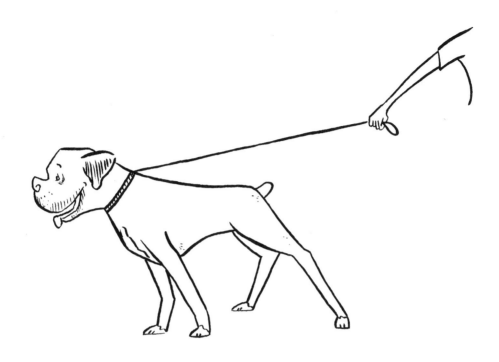

FOLLOW ME

When you are outside with your dog, whoever is in front is in charge of the adventure. For both of your sakes, it had better be you! When you take the lead, your dog can relax, relieved of her duty to protect and alert you to potential danger—including such imagined hazards as a friendly neighbor or dog. Being out front, you avoid all manner of unpleasant surprises, from sudden lunging against the leash to, worst of all, a serious dog fight.

Avoid chaos by teaching your dog one simple direction: to follow you when walking on a leash. The mere act of taking the forward position, like a pilot flying a plane, immediately elevates your status. With a few quick tugs of the leash, you become your dog's leader and guardian, with all the responsibility and authority that position entails. It is your job to make directional decisions and read the environment for potential dangers. This task is far easier than it may sound, in part because your dog will soon enjoy the relaxed feeling of camaraderie and guidance. With both of you freed from the power struggle, your walks will take on a carefree air. Now you can fully enjoy the walk—and each other's company.

Miss Sarah Says

In dog walking, as in modern architecture, form follows function. How you carry yourself is more than a social statement—it can make the difference between a pleasant excursion and a muscle-straining battle of wills.

Let's examine your walking posture. If you curl your arm too far forward, you are lifting your dog out of her natural line of gravity, in effect pulling her in front of you. This places tremendous strain on your dog's collar and leash, not to mention your shoulder and back. Maintaining a death grip on the leash is similarly pointless. Your white knuckles do not convey leadership or camaraderie—they merely threaten asphyxiation! Your dog will continue to pull, attempting to escape, and, if given the chance, will bolt. There is a better way.

Before you set out for a stroll, pack a pocket or pouch with kibble and toys. Be generous and cheerful while your dog is standing by your side, and she will want to stay there. When you are doling out goodies and remaining positive, who wouldn't want to be near you?

Finish your walk in your yard, or stop along the way to spend a few uninterrupted moments praising and playing with your dog.

Straining on the leash causes another problem. Even slight pressure can throw your dog off her center of gravity, forcing her to lean forward to maintain balance. This posture is not merely awkward. Another dog might interpret it as an aggressive challenge. When dogs meet under such circumstances, they are more likely to fight.

When you encounter unfamiliar dogs or people, teach your dog to pay attention to you and your directions instead of focusing on outside distractions. If you are unable to contain your dog's strain, you may need to purchase a head collar or some other special training device. Please consult a professional for suggestions.

When you see another person or dog approaching, instruct your dog to "Leave it." Walk with great authority, refocusing your dog with your navigational skills. If the other dog is off leash or out of control, distract or discourage your dog from making eye contact or otherwise confronting the strange dog.

There are commercial products designed to repel aggressive dogs and other animals, such as a canister spray equivalent in appearance to pepper spray, though less harmful. While this spray can be an effective tool for warding off dangerous situations, it presumes that you have a free hand and the presence of mind to react very quickly. As with driving, staying generally alert is usually the best way to avoid danger.

Miss Sarah Says

Teaching your dog to follow along at your side can be surprisingly easy. Most dogs enjoy the direction and security you provide. At first, think more of attracting your dog than leading her. Become someone she *wants* to be near! Start by winning her attention with frequent praise and treats. Then find a quiet side street or a field in which to practice the following exercise.

1. Stash your treats somewhere obvious so that your dog knows what will come her way if she cooperates.

2. Say "Follow" as you walk a few steps, and then stop.

3. If your dog stops with you, reward and congratulate her.

4. If she pulls away, let the leash go slack, and then say "Follow" again as you turn and walk in the other direction.

5. Regardless of your dog's response, congratulate her arrival back at your side. No hard feelings. She will learn to follow you to avoid being left behind.

6. Extend the distance she must follow before you reward her. Be generous with your rewards.

Gradually work your way into more open areas. Use praise and rewards to encourage her attention, refocusing her as necessary with occasional turns and tugs.

TABLE MANNERS

*E*tiquette books for humans devote entire chapters to table manners, involving complex rules for everything from seating to utensils. Happily, table manners for dogs can be reduced to one basic maxim: Eat and drink only from your bowl.

Of course, teaching your dog to act properly around his bowl or at your table is really one more way you are establishing your authority by organizing your shared living space. If your dog begs while you eat, barks impatiently as you fill his bowl, or drinks from the toilet, then you too are guilty—guilty of permitting, or perhaps even encouraging, these boorish mannerisms. Fortunately, dear reader, help is at hand.

Miss Sarah Says

If you allow your dog to loiter nearby while you are eating, you will almost certainly experience interruptions. If anyone so much as looks at him, then you have invited him to the feast! In fact, a dog will roam about and stare at everyone, quickly learning whom he can noodle for a scrap. Politely ask guests to help civilize your dog by ignoring him until the meal has ended.

To help your dog master his table manners, teach him to lie on a floor mat while you dine. The mat should be within sight of the table but well beyond reach. To prevent hunger tension, feed your dog his own meal before you sit down to enjoy yours. Then send him to his special mat, instructing him to "Settle."

If he cannot hold still, secure him on a leash and instruct "Stay." If he continues to fidget or, worse, barks, provide a satisfying chew to keep him occupied.

If you want to share leftovers, then do so in a manner unlikely to disturb your human guests. Wait until you have finished your meal, and then place a sensible portion in his bowl. He will learn to wait patiently for his share.

Are you feeling a tad guilty about eating while your dog watches? It may help to take a moment to consider his good fortune. Each of his meals is lovingly portioned and served, sparing him the rigors of a daily hunt. Your home itself is a constant comfort that eliminates his need to seek shelter. Your dog leads an enviable life.

And please remember that dogs have many more dietary limitations than humans do. Milk products and processed foods are not digested well and may lead to indigestion, gas, or diarrhea. Your dog's typical diet may appear to lack variety—until you read the label. Most high-quality dog foods are scientifically formulated to provide complete canine nutrition—something human foods can never quite accomplish.

Miss Sarah Says

When establishing your dog's mealtimes, ensure civility from the start. At first, it may seem cute that your dog greets his bowl with enthusiastic leaping and barking, but this performance soon becomes tiresome, and even embarrassing in front of company. Here is a better approach:

1. Designate a quiet spot for your dog's food and water dishes.

2. Encourage him to sit and wait as you prepare each meal.

3. If he will not cooperate, make the experience educational by securing a leash and stepping on it to prevent jumping until he has composed himself.

4. Carry his dish to his eating station and instruct "Sit."

5. Say "Okay" as you place his bowl on the floor and praise him.

6. Let everyone take part in preparing his meals, insisting that everyone follow the same routine, regardless of their age.

7. If your dog displays possessiveness when others approach his dish, you must discourage him. A good method is to shake a treat cup as you approach your dog's bowl, adding to his meal instead of removing the dish.

Note: If your dog stiffens or growls when you approach his bowl, do *not* continue. Instead, consult your veterinarian or a dog behavior specialist.

From the standpoint of civility and even safety, certain canine eating behaviors are more disturbing than others. As always, dear reader, it is best to consider each problem from your dog's perspective.

- *Toilet drinking:* Does your dog view your commode as his personal drinking fountain? Because he cannot fathom a toilet's intended purpose, he may be attracted to the cool water he finds there. You can dissuade this practice with an equally refreshing alternative: a cool bowl of water in or near the bathroom. Until he modifies this habit, it is best to keep the toilet lid closed.

- *Dinner motion:* Does your dog fidget at mealtimes, perhaps overturning his dish, carrying his kibble to another location, or racing about and eating on the run? This behavior can be mystifying until you realize that he is just following his natural drive to eat in seclusion—away from the competition of the pack. Of course, hoarding behavior is unnecessary in your home. You can promote more peaceful mealtimes by adding a little food to his dish as he dines to reassure him that you will not steal from him and that there is plenty to eat. If he continues to race about while eating, feed him in a secluded spot, perhaps in his crate, or secure him to an immovable object.

- *Gulp and swallow:* Does your dog compulsively wolf down his food? This, too, may be a way of protecting food from imaginary competition, although simple hunger may trigger the behavior. It is important to eliminate this habit, as gulping can lead to a life-threatening disorder called bloat, causing the stomach to twist and blocking circulation. To condition a more relaxed eating style, place a large rock in his bowl that he must eat around, thus pacing his mouthfuls.

NIGHTTIME RITUALS

We humans think of sleep as a passive experience, but to your dog, it is anything but. As pack animals, dogs depend upon group interaction, finding safety in numbers—especially at night, when sleeping means vulnerability. Dogs much prefer to sleep with others, be it other pets or humans. Where and how your dog sleeps can affect her attitude and behavior all day long.

Of course, many dog owners have quite different ideas about their pets' sleeping arrangements. Fortunately, there is something dogs find almost as reassuring as your presence: consistent bedtime rituals. Like people, dogs seek a cozy, familiar place to sleep. It is up to you to choose a suitable resting spot and help your dog understand and adapt to this routine.

Miss Sarah Says

As all new puppy owners discover, establishing your dog's nightly routine is essential for maintaining bedtime decorum, not to mention peace and quiet. Consistency and patience are mandatory.

Choose a quiet area in which to arrange your dog's bedding. If sharing a space with others is out of the question, choose a darkened room with few windows, lest the light of the morning and the sound of birds awaken your dog predawn. Place your dog's bedding in a corner or under a table. Think of these accommodations from her perspective: the more denlike, the better.

If traffic noise or other disruptive sounds are unavoidable, mask them with calming music. This is especially important for a young puppy, who until recently was comforted by the company of her mother and littermates. To smooth the transition, simulate a companion puppy with a towel-wrapped hot pack and a ticking clock. Such bedtime toys are available for purchase (one popular brand is Snuggle Puppies), although a handmade version will do just fine.

The darkness and solitude of night can be frightening to a dog of any age, and that is an argument for allowing your dog to sleep in your bedroom, if not in your bed. If your dog is awakened at night but can see that you are close by, she will instinctively study your reaction. Observing your peaceful slumber will calm her, and she will drift back to sleep. What's more, if she is sleeping on the floor, she will have to look up to you—a bonus opportunity to reinforce your status as team leader while you sleep.

Place a dog cushion or crate near your bedside. If your dog is restless or tempted to pace, secure her on a leash near your bed, allowing her only a few feet to stand and turn around. Think of this not as restrictive, but rather like tucking a child into bed. Given limited options, she will learn to settle down and rest at your side. After a few days or weeks, you will no longer need to secure her at night. She will develop solid sleeping patterns that will last a lifetime.

A final note on allowing your dog to sleep near you: It is by far the most reliable way to ensure that everyone gets a restful night's sleep. This is especially evident in the morning, when an isolated dog's anxiety may escalate to near-panic as she attempts to rouse you with whining, barking, or howling. By contrast, a dog who sees her human still sleeping is likely to roll over and snooze right along with you.

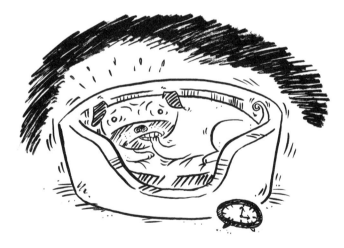

Do you find yourself asking, "Can't I just let my dog sleep in bed with me?" It is a perfectly fair question, and the answer is yes, once she is respectful of your direction and you have taught her how to ask permission. If you don't establish some ground rules first, however, she won't just share your bed; she will take it over!

To teach your dog to ask permission, direct her to sit and look to you—the canine equivalent of asking politely. Initially, deny permission at least half of the time, pointing to *her* bed on the floor as you instruct her to "Settle." When you do give her permission to join you, assign her a specific location on the bed and insist that she stay there, lest you wake to discover that *you* have been relegated to the floor.

A final word of warning: If your dog is aggressive or domineering, allowing her to sleep in your bed beside you is a bad idea. You will undermine your efforts to teach her that you are the top dog. When a dog has a challenging personality, reinforcing your leadership must remain your priority. Make every effort to reshape her contentious attitude. If you do not succeed, please seek the help of a professional trainer.

In a dog's world, those who rest in high places are revered. Therefore, if you have a puppy or a young, untrained dog, do not allow her to spend even a small portion of her day on your bed with you. Placing her on your level conveys an equality that may confuse her. Before you invite her to bed, your puppy must pass a short course in "level training."

To this end, place a crate or dog bed at your bedside and condition her to sleep at your side—but *on the floor.* Remember that in your dog's eyes, your sleeping position defines your authority. If you allow your dog to share your bed at night and then notice that she ignores your directions by day, don't say I didn't warn you!

Should your dog jump onto the bed uninvited, simply evict her with a curt "Off!" If necessary, gently flick her off with her collar or leash. Immediately direct her to "Settle" on her own space on the floor to rest or chew.

Once your dog demonstrates that she respects your rules, you can invite her onto your bed for a quick cuddle or a dream-laden slumber.

ROMPS AND RECREATION

Playful interaction is perhaps the greatest pleasure that you and your dog can share. How convenient that it is also an excellent opportunity to reinforce canine etiquette! Of course, success depends upon choosing the right games and playing them with a little extra thought and ingenuity. For example, you can encourage your dog to chase one toy while you play with another. He will want your toy and will return to you immediately, at which point you can require a "Sit," which you can reward by tossing your toy. With repetition, this game can sharpen your dog's ability to sit, fetch, and come.

Good games aren't just fun; they build a lifelong sense of trust and teamwork. Enthusiastic play helps keep your dog focused on your direction. One caveat: It is best to avoid games that can cause frustration, like prolonged sessions of keep-away. Dogs see this type of game as confrontational and competitive and quickly learn to equate "winning" with ignoring and evading your direction.

Few dogs enjoy solitary interaction. Generally speaking, a dog's concept of "play" involves two beings, regardless of their species. You might think that your dog will exercise when left alone outside, but this isolation usually creates more anxiety and tension. The best games involve others and encourage concentration and cooperation. By organizing regular, active playtimes, you are structuring your dog's view of the world—a world that usually includes you—just as your dog prefers it.

Miss Sarah Says

Use playtime to help your dog learn how to contain his impulses to jump, snatch, and grab. Here are some fun props to help facilitate your interaction and provide positive reinforcement.

- Make treat cups. Place broken treats in a cup and shake it until your dog associates the sound of the cup with getting a reward.

- Discover which toys excite your dog. Try squeaky toys, balls, flying discs, and the like. Once you find the winners, place several aside so that you and your dog are never vying for the same object!

- Dogs enjoy chasing objects on the ground. Consider indestructible balls or plastic bottles—again, always bringing more than one so that you are seen as having the most desirable toy.

Miss Sarah Says

Like children and snowflakes, every dog is unique. Your dog has a special personality all his own. Finding games that you both enjoy is the key to developing your dog's inner talents. At least one of these favorites is sure to spark your mutual enthusiasm:

- Use a treat cup to entice your dog to chase you. Demand stillness before relinquishing the goody. Use words like "Sit," "Follow," and "Come" to imprint word memory.

  Use multiple treat cups to send him from one person to the next. Give directions with your names and his: "Boomer, find Miss Sarah!" Then "Find Lindsay!" As his skills improve, expand the game to a form of hide-and-seek.

- If your dog displays an insatiable urge to tug, set up a team tug. Attach two tugging ropes to an immovable object, such as a tree trunk, and tug together. A team tug serves as a bonding ritual, whereas a game of tug-of-war between dog and human can encourage conflict or, worse, outright aggression.

- Toss multiple objects—one at a time, of course—to keep your dog interested in the game. Praise him each time he allows you to exchange a toy. Doing so will hone his sharing skills. You can also use treats as a reward for cooperation.

- Don't fling flying discs right away. At first, try rolling them. A rolling disc is much easier for a dog to grasp. As your dog shows interest and gains confidence, gradually introduce short tosses.

- If your dog delights in chasing people or other animals, refocus his passion by swinging a smooth object, such as an empty plastic bottle. To make it more enticing, smear the lid with peanut butter or cheese, encouraging him to grab and lick the contraption rather than tug it.

ON HOLIDAY

Consideration for others is the very essence of etiquette. Vacation time is no exception—especially if you are thinking of bringing along your dog. In this case, the "others" you must consider are your fellow travelers, your hosts (whether they be friends, family, or hotel employees), and, of course, your dog. Should you take your dog along? Will she be welcomed and comfortable upon your arrival? How will others react? And if she stays behind, where should you leave her? Decisions, decisions.

Miss Sarah Says

Taking your dog with you on vacation sounds lovely, but if your itinerary would condemn her to long bouts of isolation, you may do well to reconsider. Dogs do not enjoy solitude and are wary of unfamiliar surroundings. Airline travel is especially stressful because it requires both of those things—and can be risky, too.

On the other hand, if your destination is truly dog-friendly and your schedule is flexible, well, then your dog may treasure the special time with you away from home.

When you pack your dog's bags, bring as many familiar items as you can—beds, crates, gates, bowls, leashes, and toys. Surrounded by her favorite objects, she will feel more settled in her new surroundings.

If you are visiting friends or family, take along a "language list" of your dog's familiar words and routines. Hearing recognizable language will help her feel more welcome and included in the new environment.

Most people enjoy leisure travel because a short stay in a new environment offers interesting new sights, unusual entertainment, and often exotic foods. But few of these experiences are a complete surprise. In fact, we choose our destinations precisely because we know what we expect to find and enjoy. We know how we are going to get there and when we are coming back.

For a dog, however, travel is just the opposite. Having no idea what to expect, every new experience is a potential menace. What's more, your dog has no idea that vacations are temporary. As far as she knows, each short excursion means the end of life as she knows it. This can be especially true of recently adopted dogs.

So, please, consider your dog's perspective and needs before planning your trip. Can she handle the strange surroundings and unpredictability of the average vacation, or would she be happier in her own familiar setting? Consider how your dog usually reacts to new aromas, strange topography, and fresh faces. Do these things excite or distress her? Her reactions not only will affect your holiday; they may dominate it! Base your decision on what is right for your dog.

Here are some questions to ask yourself:

- Is your dog a homebody or the adventurous type?

- Does she welcome new friends or prefer trusted companions?

- Do unrecognizable scents send her into a frenzy, or has she learned to ignore them?

Remember, your dog's behavior reflects upon all dogs, not just your own. If you decide to take your dog with you on vacation, here are some tips to help you keep her calm, comfortable, and cooperative while traveling and throughout your stay:

- Long car trips can jangle a dog's nerves. If your dog becomes fidgety or boisterous in the car, she could even cause an accident. Consider such safety precautions as a harness belt, crate, or barricade, which can restrain her comfortably while traveling.

- If you are traveling in hot weather, carry an extra set of keys, enabling you to leave the air conditioning running if you're forced to leave your dog in the car for even a minute. A vehicle's interior heats very quickly in summer. Your dog can die from suffocation or heatstroke in just a few minutes.

- Plan your travel schedule and pack accordingly—including measured amounts of food, snacks, and water for every scheduled stop.

- Make a checklist so that you don't forget your dog's favorite toys and chews, her leash (and a spare!), and enough waste disposal bags for the entire trip.

If your dog is staying behind, try not to feel guilty or sad. She will be content with a stable routine and will be delighted to see you upon your return. Besides, the little surprises that frustrate adults—overheated cars, sick children, lost luggage—may prove overwhelming to your dog. Don't create a situation that makes you wish you all had stayed home.

Miss Sarah Says

Finding a dog-friendly hotel takes an extra bit of planning, but thanks to the Internet, it is easier than ever to research which hotel chains are especially welcoming to pets. You should have no trouble finding accommodations for yourself and your dog, especially in a major city. To ensure that you and your dog remain welcome, please mind her manners as well as your own. Direct her to stay at your side and follow you closely from the lobby to your room. It goes without saying that you must do all you can to protect the comfort, convenience, and privacy of your fellow guests and the hotel staff.

Upon entering your room, immediately arrange your dog's belongings at her level. Designate one area with her bedding, bowls, and toys. Next, locate the dog-walking areas and learn the hotel's rules for waste disposal.

If you are planning to leave your dog alone in the room for any length of time, exercise and feed her first. Leave the radio or TV on to drown out any unfamiliar sounds. If she is restless and prone to barking, you may have to rearrange your plans or even stay with her. Although some dog-friendly hotels have supervised kennels, many do not. It is *not* acceptable to leave a barking or howling dog behind to annoy other guests.

When you are out and about, take a reserved approach when meeting new dogs. Direct your dog to follow you, while you take cues from the other dog's handler, as well as the posture and attitude of the dog. For more tips on greeting people and dogs in public, consult the section entitled "Social Graces."

If the people you are visiting have dogs themselves, introduce the dogs in a neutral location, preferably outdoors, to avoid territorial disputes or confusion. You and your hosts should use long leashes to encourage natural interaction while allowing you to intervene if necessary—only in the case of severe confrontations or an actual dog fight.

Miss Sarah Says

Leaving your dog at home is probably harder on you than it is on her. Missing each other is only natural, but for dogs, familiarity breeds contentment. Should you choose a kennel or have a friend or professional pet sitter care for your dog in your home? Each option has its pros and cons.

- Kennels are safe and consistent—if sometimes a bit loud. Some dogs find the constant stimulation exhilarating.

- A friend or pet sitter can stay in your home or, if your dog has access to water and to his potty area, can visit three times a day for regular walks, playtime, and feeding.

    Friends are fine unless your dog's behavior amounts to a major imposition. In that case, a pet sitter may be a better option.

- Hiring a pet sitter may seem ideal, but check references! Your daily routine may be difficult for a stranger to replicate.

    Be sure to write down clear instructions for your dog's daily schedule, including where in your home to find extra food, snacks, toys, and waste disposal bags. On a separate sheet, list your emergency contact information and prepare and sign a letter of authorization in case your dog needs veterinary care. Make three copies: one set for you, one for the sitter, and one to post in your house for easy reference.

Holidays are never stress-free, but by providing familiar surroundings and daily structure, you can make your dog as comfortable as possible.

SOCIAL GRACES

A dog who looks and listens to direction and has learned to keep his nose to himself is almost universally welcomed. But those are just the basics. This section addresses the finer points of canine civility—from being a good neighbor to meeting others to entertaining.

In many ways, dog etiquette is as simple as the Golden Rule. Would you want to live next door to a dog who barks excessively while ardently patrolling the perimeter of his property? Although I hate to burst this dog's bubble, his fierce barking is not scaring away those passing pedestrians. They had no intention of visiting in the first place.

If you are lucky enough to have your own yard, do not permit your dog to dig holes. After all, he is defacing not just your yard, but also your neighbor's view of it. Although digging is a natural canine behavior, you can prevent it by confining your dog to a specific area and redirecting him to less-destructive pastimes. Avoid prolonged bouts of isolation, as these promote boredom, which is where most mischief begins. Most important, you must control and prevent any aggressive or threatening behavior that your dog may exhibit. Once a survival skill, canine aggression today is not merely antisocial, but dangerous to your social standing and, in these litigious times, to your life's savings. If your dog has violent tendencies, you must take full responsibility for curbing such behavior.

Miss Sarah Says

Does your dog exhibit any of the aforementioned unacceptable behaviors? If not, congratulations! You are already raising an ambassador of canine etiquette. But if your dog resorts to such destructive forms of entertainment as digging or hair-trigger barking, examine your role in perpetuating these behaviors. Are you interacting regularly, or are you allowing your dog to become lonely and bored? Are you reinforcing the proper behaviors? Indeed, how can you tell?

The first step is to examine and improve your routine. Analyze your dog's schedule as thoroughly as you would a child's. Organize his feedings and outings, and set aside time to teach him new words or routines, leaving time each day for free play and fun. The section "Romps and Recreation" offers good advice on the most appropriate games. Do not leave your dog outside for extended periods; limit outdoor activities to when you can interact with him. Indoor isolation (up to four hours) is preferable to outdoor freedom that is neither shared nor directed.

If you need to be away for longer periods, hire a dog walker or ask a family member or friend to drop by. Ask your veterinarian for reliable referrals.

I realize that barking is often a dog's only way to vent frustration or convey emotion. It is natural to sympathize, but it is important to be consistent in directing his behavior. And while it is frustrating when his bad behavior persists, yelling at a dog is almost never effective. Your dog interprets human shouting as a form of competitive or playful barking. Rather than settle down, he will be all too delighted to chime in. Whereas humans can learn to contain frustration and exercise patience, your dog may not be able to.

Note: If you must leave a dog outside unattended, take care to address his physical needs. Provide shelter from bad weather or, if it is hot and sunny, a source of shade or even a shallow wading pool. Make sure to leave a large, tip-proof bowl of water, along with an assortment of beloved toys and a few favorite chews. A dog left tethered to a post will quickly become lonely and anxious, or worse, will begin to develop aggressive tendencies.

Your dog believes, "I bark, therefore I am." You can redirect his energy toward social interaction until he concludes, "We are together, therefore I am." Here is a useful sequence for controlling your dog's barking:

Attach a lightweight leash to his regular collar. If necessary, add a head collar.

Strategically place treat cups around your home. The moment you see your dog become excited, get a treat cup, and then walk behind him calmly and lift the leash discreetly.

Tug back on the leash emphatically and say "Shhhh." The instant your dog looks to you, switch gears quickly: Run back a few paces as you shake the cup and call his name.

When he returns to your side, praise him and give him a treat. Encourage him to remain alongside you by walking away as you say "Follow," shaking the treat cup and offering treats to him as you walk along.

As your dog begins to cooperate, you can let him drag his leash or give him full freedom to wander your home. Soon, your dog will bark to alert you and then race to find you. Good dog!

Most dogs find sheer joy in digging up cool dirt on a warm day. Your dog probably finds it mystifying that you do not share in his pleasure, and is further baffled that you take such pride in manicuring your topography. For this reason, you must take great measures to limit your dog's unsupervised accessibility to your yard until he learns to redirect his habit.

Miss Sarah Says

If your dog loves to dig and cannot control his obsession, you will need to provide a consistent outlet, along with some creative discouragement.

- Consider designating a spot near your home or on your property for your dog to dig. Direct him to the area by saying "Go dig." Join in the activity at first, either with a shovel or with your hands, to reinforce your approval.

- A more refined, but costlier, solution is a child's sandbox. Hide toys and bones in the sand, directing your dog to "Go dig" each time you commence this activity.

- To discourage digging in undesirable locations, bury your dog's old stools and some red pepper in shallow holes, covering each hole with dirt and a large rock.

In the wild, dogs have no greater joy than running down prey—a pleasure denied them in urban settings, where live game is difficult to come by. Too often, these hunting and herding instincts are displaced onto hapless passersby, whether they travel by car or bicycle or on sneakers.

You must squelch this unacceptable behavior immediately, before your dog harms himself or, worse, harms someone else. Redirect him with a game of makeshift soccer, allowing him to burn off energy as he satisfies his hunting instinct by capturing the ball or an empty plastic soda bottle. For other appropriate displacement activities, refer to the section "Romps and Recreation."

Miss Sarah Says

If your dog likes to chase, you have no alternative but to teach him not to. Until he learns, you must limit his access to the street and closely monitor his interactions with visitors and passersby.

Create learning exercises by placing him on a teaching collar and leash. Expose him to distractions while you watch him closely. The moment he drops his head, body, or ears in preparation to dart forth, pull back and say "No." Direct him to "Sit-Stay" and brace him if necessary. When possible, redirect his attention with a toy.

If you have children, ask them to run around in front of your dog while you manage the leash. The moment he hunkers down for the chase, pull back and say "No." Redirect him to "Stay" as the children continue to dart about until he accepts or ignores their motion. When you release him to play, ask the children to toss or kick a ball. That way, your dog can enjoy the interaction even as you redirect his chasing impulse to toys rather than people.

MEETING AND GREETING

It takes skill to put others at ease. This holds true for both humans and dogs. Help your dog make a positive and lasting first impression so that your new acquaintances will want to see you both again.

To eliminate jumping, mouthing, or pawing, teach your dog to sit before greeting others. This posture will earn him the attention he craves, in a manner that is socially acceptable. As always, consider your dog's point of view. Would your dog enjoy a child running up to him, clawing at his coat for recognition? I should think not!

Miss Sarah Says

Never allow your dog to drag you along just because he is eager to greet others. This behavior is as unsafe as it is impolite. Were his leash to break, a catastrophic incident could result. Teach your dog the proper protocol with this technique:

1. When approaching another person or dog, instruct your dog to "Follow" at your side.

2. Before greetings commence, instruct "Sit."

3. If your dog does not obey, position him by gently squeezing his waist muscles and bracing his chest as you pet him. To brace him, clip your thumb over his collar and, if necessary, steady his waist.

4. Instruct your dog to "Stay" and invite the onlooker's affections. Praise your dog if he remains still. If he wiggles or attempts to jump, remind him with a gentle "Shhhh!"

Greeting another canine confronts your dog with an overwhelming array of scents and sensations that we humans can scarcely appreciate. Help him contain his excitement. Teach him never to strain against the leash. Other dogs often mistake the resulting forward-leaning posture for naked aggression. If the other dog is also on a leash, he will counter-posture merely to hold his ground. This can quickly lead to escalating hostilities, even between two dogs who might otherwise get along fine were they off-leash.

Always focus your dog on your own authority. Encourage him to jog at your side until you are close enough to the other dog for them to interact on loose leashes. If his straining proves too difficult to manage, consider a head collar or other teaching aid to ensure your control.

Miss Sarah Says

When introducing two dogs, courtesy counts. Even as you direct your own dog's behavior, be mindful of the other dog's posture and comportment.

As the dogs approach one another, each should walk at his person's side. Once you are close enough to meet and greet, ask the other person whether her dog is friendly and would like to meet your dog. If the answer is no, politely lead your dog in another direction. After all, some dogs simply don't like others of their species.

If the answer is yes, lessen the tension on your dog's leash and give your dog permission to leave your side with the direction "Okay, go play!"

If the oncoming dog is ill-behaved, you have no excuse for abandoning your own principles. If your dog responds impulsively, remind him to "Follow" or brace him at your side.

If you are approached by an off-leash dog, keep to yourself and encourage your dog to do the same. No matter what the other dog's reaction, walk on as if he weren't there. Avoid speeding up, as any reaction from you, *including eye contact,* may be interpreted as a confrontation. By remaining calm and keeping your dog on track, you can ensure that your retreat from his perceived territory will be viewed as submissive and respectful. He can safely ignore you and reserve his aggression for a more formidable foe.

It may be a time-honored canine ritual, but etiquette demands that you prevent your dog from greeting people by sniffing their crotches. As a practical matter, this behavior is almost never reciprocated, and if it is, then dog etiquette is the least of your social problems.

Clearly, you must teach your dog more acceptable ways to welcome visitors. But first, a word about people who simply dislike or fear dogs, or are allergic to them. Courtesy requires that you respect your guests' wishes and do all you can to keep your dog away from them.

For dogs who have learned to stay quietly away from company, this directive poses no problem. If your dog becomes highly stressed by isolation, however, arrange for a play date in another household, or tire him out before guests arrive and then place him in his sleeping area with a radio playing to drown out the sounds of your interactions.

Miss Sarah Says

If your dog is an ardent crotch-sniffer, he requires prompt rehabilitation. Enlist the help of a family member or friend—a *good* friend—and practice the following greeting ritual:

1. Manage your dog with his leash while greeting company at the door.

2. Ask your recruit to come to the door. Instruct your dog to stand behind you as you open the door, positioning him if he will not cooperate. Tell your dog to "Say hello" as you hold your visitor's hand to his nose.

3. If your dog leans in farther, edging toward the visitor's pelvis, stop him in his tracks. Say "No" as you tug back on the leash.

4. Remind your dog to "Say hello" once more as you show him your visitor's hand. If necessary, dab the visitor's hand with peanut butter to encourage sniffing. Your consistent direction will communicate that the hand is the only body part your dog is permitted to sniff.

5. Repeat this lesson as needed until the new habit takes hold.

ENTERTAINING

While you are entertaining visitors, please encourage your dog to keep his nose away from the guests and their refreshments. These same rules apply if he is fortunate enough to be invited along to a barbecue or picnic. Maintain your dog's social graces and he will remain a welcome addition to your social scene.

To ensure your dog's proper behavior, it pays to be prepared. Pack a "bag-to-go" with measured portions of his dog food, along with dishes for food and water. Also bring a pet bed or mat, as well as extra treats, toys, and a bone to chew. And don't forget a supply of waste disposal bags and paper towels to clean up any messes.

Miss Sarah Says

It is essential that your dog understand the no-plate rule, the key word being "No!" The concept of "No," however, is best communicated not through volume but through timing. Follow these instructions:

1. Rehearse with your dog by placing a tray of cheese and crackers on a low coffee table just before the party.

2. Walk him into the room on a leash.

3. The moment he alerts to the food on the table, tug him back, saying "No."

4. Say "Bad cheese, bad crackers!" as you admonish the food, not the dog.

Never yell at your dog in these situations. He will interpret your reaction as prize envy and will sneak the food when you are not looking. Instead, convince your dog that the food is bad, and that you are just warning him of this fact.

TOWN AND COUNTRY

*W*hether you are exploring the city or the country with your dog, her manners will be put to the test. She must simultaneously ignore temptations and obey your instructions despite a variety of distractions.

If you have a country dog who is not used to the pace and volume of urban life, she may be reluctant even to exit the car. Your response will shape her experience. Stay relaxed and give plenty of direction. It is generally easier for a city dog to adapt to the country, but sudden freedom to explore wide-open spaces can also cause confusion and stress.

Many of your dog's adventures begin with a car ride, so what better place to start rewarding your dog's good behavior? Just as you have assigned your dog special spaces in your home, your dog needs a designated car spot, equipped with a familiar mat, toys, and safety restraint, such as a crate or harness. Dogs cannot be permitted to jump from seat to seat and should be forbidden from climbing into the driver's lap. Doing so is not merely annoying; it threatens the safety of all the occupants of the car. What's more, fidgeting in the car is an ominous predictor of how your dog will behave upon your arrival.

Insist on your dog's relaxed cooperation as you enter, exit, and, of course, drive your car. If you arrive at your destination with your dog in a state of agitation, your fate is sealed. Consider turning around and going home.

Miss Sarah Says

Safe driving requires your full attention. Therefore, any automotive antics on your dog's part are not merely rude, but also dangerous. If she can't lie still in her assigned place, you must crate her or secure her with a car harness. In either case, provide a familiar blanket for her physical comfort. If she continues to fidget, bring along a favorite toy or bone—the dog equivalent of a child's coloring book or a handheld computer game.

Should your dog be prone to carsickness, cover her area with a sheet that can be washed later, and bring plenty of paper towels to simplify clean-ups.

Finally, note that airbags pose the same risks to dogs as they do to small children. The best place for a dog to ride is either in the back seat or in the cargo area of an SUV or a station wagon.

ABOUT TOWN

To your dog, a heavily populated location is nothing short of an olfactory amusement park. Her visual senses will also be pushed into overdrive, especially if she is unaccustomed to car travel or large crowds of people. She may express her nervousness with sudden straining at the leash or by urinating on every pillar and post. Eliminating such uncouth outbursts is up to you.

As always, require your dog to look to you for direction—literally to "Follow" your lead. Others will quickly recognize you as a team, and you will soon be assimilated into the social scene.

Miss Sarah Says

A good test of your dog's composure on a trip is how she exits the automobile. If she leaps out in a boorish tumble of excitement, she will likely be difficult to contain and control when meeting others. To ensure yourselves of a more pleasant experience, take charge from the moment you open the car door.

1. Instruct your dog to "Wait" before exiting the car.

2. Hold your dog in her seat until she is focused.

3. Darting out the door is not permitted. If she jumps from the car impulsively, she may dart into oncoming traffic. Tell her "No," place her back in the car, and begin again.

4. Release her from the automobile with the direction "Okay."

5. Immediately direct her to your side, calling her name and saying "Follow."

Miss Sarah Says

Whether you and your dog are in the city or in the country, remember that whoever is in front organizes the excursion. Make sure that the leader is *you*. Especially when visiting new places, you are your dog's guardian and protector. Walk forth with confidence.

In addition to "Follow," your basic vocabulary should include the directions "Wait-Okay," "Under," and "Back."

- *Wait-Okay:* Use these two words to guide your dog about town. Each time you encounter a curb, a stairway, or another person, ask your dog to "Wait" and focus her attention on you. Darting is poor form. If you are entering a building, use "Wait-Okay" at the door. By laying claim to the leadership role, you will take charge of the entire experience.

- *Under:* This direction instructs your dog to lie under your legs, chair, or table while you are seated. Guide her with kibble and instruct her to "Stay." You may offer a chew as you would offer a child a coloring book. Although your dog may fidget or whine, do not acknowledge her until she settles. She will learn quickly what wins your attention and will repeat that behavior.

- *Back:* If your dog steps out or pulls in front of you, simply instruct "Back" as you tug her behind you. You lead, she follows. Every time.

When you and your dog are confronted by unknown persons or pets, it is important to appear confident, even if you are feeling apprehensive or befuddled. Your air of authority and calmness will greatly reassure your dog and will help her focus on your commands.

If your dog wanders out in front of you, instruct her to "Get back!" If she is overstimulated, brace her with your free hand. Think of yourself as the pilot of an airliner in turbulence. You want to reassure your passengers, but also command them to take their seats and buckle up. In other words, you are in charge.

If your dog exhibits overt aggression, take her home and consult a professional. Aggressive behavior is a complex topic requiring a complete response that is beyond the scope of this discussion.

IN THE COUNTRY

A country excursion brings the sheer delight of open space and refreshing smells. The freedom will thrill you both, but temptations may be irresistible to your four-footed friend. Teach her to keep you within sight and work on her impulse control to keep her predatory impulses in check.

Before you venture to an open environment, practice your dog's basic directions, such as "Stay" and "Come," to ensure her responsiveness. To provide controlled freedom, take her to an enclosed yard, field, or playground (during off-hours, please) or work with her on a line that is 25 to 50 feet long, depending on the size and speed of your dog. As you walk about, reinforce your togetherness with treats and praise.

Miss Sarah Says

When planning an open-air jaunt with your dog, ask yourself a few questions:

- Will your dog obediently respond to you each time you beckon? If not, pack a long line to ensure her safety.

- Is your dog physically able to keep pace with you and manage the terrain? If not, you must reassess and revise your travel plans.

- Is the environment dog-friendly and safe? What hazards are posed by nearby water, burrs, wildlife, or hunters? Think carefully before including your dog. Her safety depends on your good judgment.

- Does your destination allow dogs? Never presume; ask even if you have visited the location before. After all, rules can change.

One of the most basic—and challenging—canine commands is "Come." You have probably been saying this to your dog since she was a puppy. "Come here," "Come on," "Come along"—all variations are equal. What you hope is that your dog will stop instantaneously and then race to you enthusiastically. Of course, few humans could live up to the same expectation, but this is what you are asking of your dog.

Don't expect your dog to come just because you say so. She will learn more quickly if you offer snacks and show your cheerful appreciation. A dog who is welcomed back to your side with praise and goodies is far more likely to stay close by.

If your dog's response to the direction "Come" is a bit iffy, practice it often and with gusto. Never punish a negative reaction; doing so is pointless, even counterproductive. Do you really think that angry shouting will make your dog want to come closer?

To your dog, the word "Come" has the same connotation as the word "Huddle!" Think of yourself and your dog as a team: You're only going to win by sticking together. You are the captain, leading with insight, praise, and rewards.

And let us not forget the importance of controlling your eye contact. When calling your dog, stare at her only *after* she has returned to your side. Otherwise, she will mistake your gaze for approval and interpret it as permission to wander as she pleases. Rehearse "Come" with the following games:

- *Name Toss:* Practice saying your dog's name as you turn your head away from her. Your trailing voice is far more enticing than repeatedly calling her as you chase her down.

- *Look What I Found:* Pretend to find something wonderful on the ground, or play with one of your dog's favorite toys. If you appear interested, she will be, too!

- *Right Here:* When you beckon to your dog, either move away from her or kneel down, point, and stare at the exact spot you'd like her to occupy. When she reaches the target, praise her extravagantly.

If you want to add a spark to your dog's training adventures, find a little handheld device known as a clicker. When you pair its sharp sound with a tempting food reward, your dog will make a positive connection to the noise. With this sequence guaranteed, the combination of click and reward will ensure that all highlighted performances are repeated. A clicker is invaluable when teaching your dog to come when called (see the next page for a series of helpful exercises), although it can be used to teach other routines as well.

Be cheerful and have fun as you click and reward all important behaviors: going potty in the designated spot, behaving politely with company, learning to lie down at your request, walking cooperatively, and coming to you when called. Think of the clicker's sound as capturing a snapshot of a moment you would like to see repeated, using it to spotlight your dog's cooperation.

Miss Sarah Says

Here are several ways to use your clicker to reinforce the direction "Come." Place your clicker and a healthy supply of treats or kibble in a fanny pack or pocket. Click the moment your dog returns to you—never while you are still apart.

- Take your dog into a fenced enclosure or play with her on a long line so that she may enjoy considerable freedom. Each time she chooses to come near you, click and reward her. In short order, you will notice that she returns with predictable regularity.

- If your dog shows no interest in coming near you, do something to lure her: Play with a favorite toy or stick, sniff the ground as if you've found something fascinating, or shake a treat cup and pretend to be eating the snacks rather than luring her. Do not look at or plead with her, as your eye contact will reward her independence and reinforce your separation. Instead, make yourself the constant object of your dog's focus by acting busy and entertained. Click and reward your dog the moment she returns to your side, saying "Come" only *after* you have reunited. You want your dog to learn that "Come" means you are together, not apart.

- Running away from your dog is another great lure, especially if you are waving a treat, toy, or stick. Shout your praise as you play keep-away. When you turn to embrace your dog, click and reward her as you say "Come!"

Although visiting the Great Outdoors may suggest unlimited freedom for your dog, it comes with an added burden of social responsibility. Leaving natural resources and wildlife habitats unspoiled is not a mere courtesy; often, it is also the law. Whether you are visiting a farm, a park, or a nature preserve, be sure to follow all posted rules.

Wide-open spaces may prove irresistible to your dog, so it is especially important to keep her in check. Farm animals and wildlife can be dangerous if provoked. After all, they aren't waiting around longing for you and your dog to visit them. If your dog cannot reliably return each time she is called, you must keep her on a long leash.

Treat encounters with wildlife the way you would encounters with other dogs: Be mindful of their body language as well as your dog's posture. But unless the other animal is another dog, stay a healthy distance away.

A note to those with small breeds: Please be especially careful outdoors and keep your dog close on a leash. Otherwise, there is a very real risk that she could end up as a quick snack for a fox, eagle, or coyote. Many small dogs are unaware of their relative size. As a result, each year hundreds of dog owners are devastated by such savage attacks. Your small dog's safety is your responsibility.

Miss Sarah Says

If you are unsure how your dog will react to people, wildlife, or other dogs, keep her on a long leash. It will allow for exploration and play while ensuring your dog's safety. Now you have the means to restrain your dog if she is startled or begins to wander off:

1. Calmly pick up the long line or strengthen your hold on the leash.

2. Call your dog as you throw your voice in the opposite direction.

3. Run a few paces to encourage your dog to leave the distraction and stay with you.

4. If she ignores you, say "No" as you allow the slack in the leash to tighten. Then, if you must, reel her to your side.

Once she is back at your side, do not express anger or admonish her, or she won't want to be near you the next time. Your goal is to encourage togetherness in all situations.

AIN'T MISBEHAVIN'

*D*oes your dog act out or dismantle your home when life does not meet his expectations? If he is prone to fidgeting when bored or anxious, his behavior is a good indicator of his state of mind. Although your dog is unaware of how his routines affect your mood, you can control your response to teach him more appropriate activities. Misbehavior is rarely a sign of deliberate mischief. It indicates an eager dog who simply has nothing else to satisfy his craving for activity. Redirecting your dog's impulsive behavior is paramount in restoring civility to your household.

Miss Sarah Says

Just because you find some of your dog's behaviors irksome does not mean that he is misbehaving. If his actions satisfy an urge or capture your attention, then it is perfectly logical for him to repeat them. Try to think of "problem" behaviors as proof of your dog's intelligence—and be grateful for the teaching opportunities they provide.

Create an environment in which encouragement far exceeds admonishment. For every behavior you discourage, promote another behavior in its place:

- A dog who nips can be taught to lick instead.

- A jumper can be taught to sit or fetch when greeting others.

- A chewer can be provided with suitable bones or toys to gnaw on to his heart's content.

A healthy displacement activity can occupy time and energy that might otherwise be spent destroying valuables or interrupting visits or family time.

Distressed Departures

Dogs can be very upset by sudden separation from those who mean the most to them. Adolescent dogs especially crave group interaction. The reasons are partly biological. You see, long before dogs became domesticated, adult wolves ventured forth from the den to scout for sustenance while puppies stayed behind, chaperoned by relatives. Between 7 and 9 months of age, however, hormones signaled that it was time for the young dogs to join the group effort. So being excluded from your activities works against your dog's very instincts. Your dog can learn to adjust to daily separation; it just doesn't come naturally.

Since your dog cannot always accompany you, it is imperative that you work to improve his waiting skills. If anxiety strikes while you are out, it may be marked by destructive chewing, house-soiling, or manic greeting rituals. Separation anxiety is natural in adolescent dogs, but it may escalate and linger if it is not handled properly.

Miss Sarah Says

Correcting your dog's mischief after the fact will not reassure him the next time you leave. If you come home to an anxiety-related incident, try not to react. Clean up all messes discreetly and without fanfare—preferably out of his sight. Here are some ways to help your dog overcome his problem behaviors:

- Review and rehearse his basic skills, such as "Follow," "Sit-Stay," "Come," and "Paw." These directions remind him that you are his leader, a thought that will comfort him when you depart.

- Exercise him more frequently, especially before a long period of isolation. Active dogs sleep more soundly.

- Pretend to leave, gathering your coat and keys and bustling around the house. Repeat this staged departure *without actually leaving* until your dog learns to ignore this ritual.

Your arrivals and departures should be similarly nonchalant, regardless of how your dog behaves. When you return from an outing, ignore your dog's emotional outbursts. The goal is for your dog to rest or chew while you are out, not to quake at the door awaiting your return.

Isolation in a crate or a small room can be just the thing to settle an anxious dog. Displacement activities, such as chewing a favorite bone or toy, are ideal distractions to absorb his anxious energy.

STOOL SWALLOWERS

Let's take a moment to address a topic not normally discussed in polite company: *coprophagia,* or stool swallowing. As distasteful as it is for humans to hear, dogs view these deposits as a delicacy. In fact, just the scent can send a dog into a ravenous frenzy. When you interfere or admonish him, he usually views your interference as competition for a limited prize, prompting him to gobble up even more droppings, thus turning a puppy's bad habit into a long-term addiction. Fortunately, there are effective ways to discourage this practice.

Miss Sarah Says

Here are some effective methods for discouraging a dog's stool-eating habit:

- If you observe that the stool-eating generally occurs at a particular time of day, that's a good time to place your dog on a long dragging leash or a retractable leash. The moment your dog looks intently at the feces, tug the leash sharply, and then divert his attention to an enticing game or a toy.

- Never clean up a dog's stools in front of a stool-eater. He may view this activity as competition or implied permission. That is, if you can make stools disappear, then why can't he?

- Pet stores and veterinary practices can sell you a food additive that makes stools less attractive to dogs. Who knew that such a thing existed?

NIPPING

The most common misconception about puppies is that nipping is a naughty behavior. Nipping is as natural for a puppy as crying is for a human baby. In fact, like a baby's cry, a puppy's nip conveys distress. Recognizing this tendency reveals numerous teaching opportunities.

Just as a parent must interpret a baby's cry in order to meet the appropriate need, dog owners must try to discover what is prompting a puppy's nipping behavior. A wise dog owner soon learns when the puppy needs to be fed, pottied, or played with—and responds accordingly.

Sadly, some dog owners physically punish their puppies for nipping, which is as pointless and cruel as spanking a baby for crying. If the puppy is scolded or punished, he will interpret the rough treatment as confrontational play. The sad result is that a good-natured puppy may develop aggressive traits that last a lifetime.

Miss Sarah Says

Responding to a puppy's nips with retaliation will confuse him. Shaking him or clamping his jaws together with your hand is not merely uncivilized—it is pointless, cruel, and *completely ineffective*. A young puppy's nips are not aggressive; they are instinctive cries for attention that call for a reassuring response. A puppy will nip most when he is overtired or needs to defecate.

One useful tool is a chart that reminds everyone in the household of the dog's daily needs. If the whole family commits to using the same commands at the same times of day, your dog will learn routines faster and will even initiate the process to get your attention.

Need	Word(s)	Routine
Eat	Hungry	Schedule feeding times. Place the bowl in the same spot, and encourage "Sit" before feeding.
Drink	Water	Keep the bowl in the same spot. Encourage "Sit."
Potty	Outside/Papers and Get Busy	Follow the same route, to the same spot. Use a bell to encourage a signal. Restrict attention until the pup eliminates.
Rest	On Your Mat or Time for Bed	Designate an area in each shared room. Provide a mat and toys; secure a leash if necessary.
Play	Bone, Ball, or Toy and Go Play	Establish a play area inside and out; make sure all four paws are on the floor before you toss a toy or give a bone.

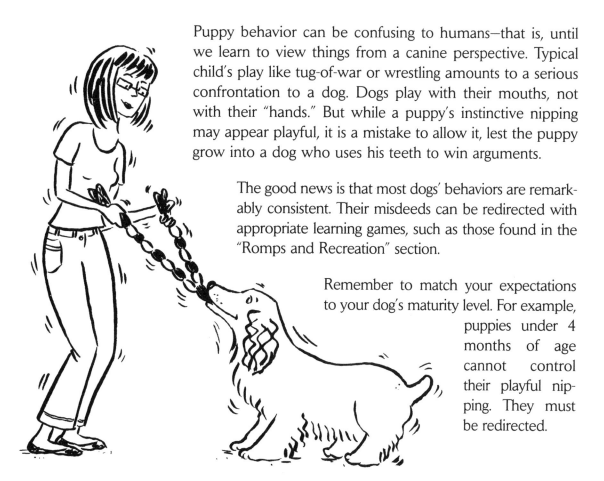

Puppy behavior can be confusing to humans—that is, until we learn to view things from a canine perspective. Typical child's play like tug-of-war or wrestling amounts to a serious confrontation to a dog. Dogs play with their mouths, not with their "hands." But while a puppy's instinctive nipping may appear playful, it is a mistake to allow it, lest the puppy grow into a dog who uses his teeth to win arguments.

The good news is that most dogs' behaviors are remarkably consistent. Their misdeeds can be redirected with appropriate learning games, such as those found in the "Romps and Recreation" section.

Remember to match your expectations to your dog's maturity level. For example, puppies under 4 months of age cannot control their playful nipping. They must be redirected.

Miss Sarah Says

If your dog's nipping seems to be growing more aggressive, you may be guilty of encouraging these tendencies through confrontational games, which challenge his strength and his will. Here are some good ways to extinguish this habit:

- When your puppy nips, you ask yourself if he might need anything. Like a crying infant, a puppy may nip to signal the need for food, water, a nap, or a potty break.

- Teach your dog to give "Kisses" by encouraging licking instead of nipping. Whenever his mouthiness escalates, try spreading butter or peanut butter on your hands. This is a good technique to teach to children—but only with adult supervision. If your dog continues to nip at children, they need to be separated until he learns to suppress that behavior.

- If all else fails, you can crate your dog—not as a form of discipline, but to calm him. If exhaustion has set in, being crated will settle him down immediately.

GRAB AND GO: THE CANINE VERSION OF KEEP-AWAY

If your dog can easily entice you to play a spontaneous game of keep-away, then you, dear reader, have been dog-trained. Dogs will repeat this game over and over simply to get your attention, and it's no wonder! It is a game that almost no human can win. Dogs seem to find new exhilaration each time they escape with one of your most prized objects.

Can you follow the strategy? The dog grabs a sock, waving it in front of his people to make sure that he has everyone's attention. Perhaps he'll even act as though he will give it back, but then he quickly turns and darts away. Pivot! Fake left! Points are awarded based on how long the game continues, how many people get involved, and how much atten-tion he gets in the end. The game has unlimited canine appeal and is an effective attention-getting ritual. It sure beats listening to the clock tick!

Since you cannot win a dog's game of keep-away, you have only two options: change the rules or change the game.

The biggest rule change is to just say "No" to keep-away. The lesson here is impulse control: Your dog must understand that keep-away is to be avoided. Because most dogs learn the word "No" as an interaction, not as an instruction, you must emphasize that there is something wrong with this game, and not with him.

A more manageable approach is to teach a substitute game. Grab-and-Show turns keep-away on its head, making it a game of shared activity and cooperation. Instead of running away with household items, your dog will learn to deliver them to you, sharing objects rather than destroying them.

GRAB-AND-SHOW

Trying to teach your dog to refrain from mouthing objects is about as hopeless as asking a toddler not to touch anything. You can meet your dog halfway, however, by teaching him to show you the objects he has found and share them with you when prompted. The Grab-and-Show game will satisfy your dog's oral fixations as well as his need for attention.

If your dog has become addicted to the game of keep-away, teaching him to share his treasure may be a challenge, although the lure of food and attention can be a sufficient reward, I assure you. In the end, this game will be as much fun, and can even help you tidy your home!

To teach your dog to relinquish objects, take him into a small room (a bathroom will do) and drop a toy. When he picks it up, encourage him to show you what he's found with a familiar phrase such as "What did you find?" as you kneel down and cheer or shake a treat cup. Each time your dog grabs and delivers an object to you, reward him with treats and plenty of affection. Then set up the bathroom with items that your dog is more likely to steal, such as socks or shoes, and repeat the exercise. Now you've shaped a cooperative skill from an annoying habit—good job!

Note: Always store valuable objects out of the reach of puppies and young dogs. Like children, puppies are tempted by anything new, especially if it is something you handle frequently.

Miss Sarah Says

If your dog still instigates keep-away, affix a lightweight 4-foot leash to his collar to enable quick and calm intervention. Prepare a treat cup and then rehearse the following situation:

1. Strategically drop an item, such as a sock, in an open room.

2. When your dog grabs it, shake the treat cup as you have rehearsed, encouraging him to "Share it." Your dog may be more than a bit confused.

3. If he attempts to bolt, maneuver yourself to the end of the leash and step on it. Do not run him down like a bug in the kitchen, however; doing so will have the obvious adverse effects.

4. Kneel down and cheerfully exchange the object in his mouth for a snack.

5. Continue to practice until your dog shares objects willingly. Gradually move the routine into all of your living spaces, making extra treat cups and stashing them within easy reach around your home.

Does it seem strange to reward a dog's "stealing" with a treat? It shouldn't, once you realize that you are simply redirecting a naturally occurring behavior. All dogs will mouth interesting objects—that is a given. Fighting this impulse only strengthens the desire to grasp and protect the treasure. Instead, teach your dog to show you his findings. Remember, to your dog, each find is of equal value. Would you rather he show your possessions or destroy them? The choice is yours.

The Concept of "No"

"No! No! No!" How many times have you found yourself repeating that word? Most dogs respond as though their names are called. This reaction does not signal understanding.

Your dog has no idea what "No" means, no matter how loudly or angrily you shout it. Although your dog will make every effort to please you, you erode that all-important trust when you communicate your displeasure so poorly. All a dog can do is react with puzzlement or fear.

The goal is to use "No" to discourage a specific activity, so it is necessary to issue this direction properly and sparingly. Never shout the word "No," and try not to repeat it. Shouting at a dog overwhelms him, and repetition is annoying and confusing. Also, remember your dog's need to feel involved. Always offer an alternative activity for his engagement. Here is a reference chart:

Discourage	Encourage
Jump on visitors	Fetch a toy or sit for pats
Nip	Lick
Grab and go	Grab and show
Bark, bark, bark	Bark once, then run to you
Chew on the furniture	Chew on a bone
Mount a leg	Grab a chew toy
Run away	Run to you

Miss Sarah Says

"No" should convey that something is wrong with the environment, not with your dog. Remember to teach "No" as a lesson like any other. Don't allow your frustration to come through in your voice or manner. Schedule regular practice, affix your dog's teaching collar and leash, and use specific objects to focus his attention. Try this exercise:

1. When your dog is elsewhere, lay a treasured temptation, such as a sock, in the middle of the floor.

2. Walk your dog on his leash and teaching collar to the sock. The moment he alerts to it, pull back on the leash and say "No."

3. Now shout at the sock without addressing your dog—reinforce the idea that something is wrong with the object. Direct your displeasure toward the sock, not your dog, to indicate that this object is to be avoided.

4. Now try this same routine with other inanimate temptations including food, countertops, and waste paper baskets.

Take care not to overwhelm your dog. Teaching "No" works only if you catch him during the thought process. It is *not* effective when you catch him in the act or after he has destroyed an item. By then, you are too late—and your overreaction will only serve to confuse him.

INDEX